**W9-CKH-144**

ECUADOR

SOUTH AMERICA TODAY

ECUADOR

Colleen Madonna Flood Williams

Mason Crest Publishers
Philadelphia

Produced by OTTN Publishing, Stockton, N.J.

Mason Crest Publishers
370 Reed Road
Broomall, PA 19008
www.masoncrest.com

First printing

1 3 5 7 9 8 6 4 2

Library of Congress Cataloging-in-Publication Data

Williams, Colleen Madonna Flood.
  Ecuador / Colleen Madonna Flood Williams.
      p. cm. — (South America today)
  Includes index.
  ISBN 978-1-4222-0636-2 (hardcover) — ISBN 978-1-4222-0703-1 (pbk.)
  1. Ecuador—Juvenile literature. [1. Ecuador.] I. Title.
  F3708.5.W55 2008
  986.6—dc22
                                        2008033555

SOUTH AMERICA
TODAY

Argentina		Paraguay
Bolivia	**South America:**	Peru
Brazil	Facts & Figures	Suriname
Chile	Ecuador	Uruguay
Colombia	Guyana	Venezuela

Table of Contents

Discovering South America

James D. Henderson

South America is a cornucopia of natural resources, a treasure house of ecological variety. It is also a continent of striking human diversity and geographic extremes. Yet in spite of that, most South Americans share a set of cultural similarities. Most of the continent's inhabitants are properly termed "Latin" Americans. This means that they speak a Romance language (one closely related to Latin), particularly Spanish or Portuguese. It means, too, that most practice Roman Catholicism and share the Mediterranean cultural patterns brought by the Spanish and Portuguese who settled the continent over five centuries ago.

Still, it is never hard to spot departures from these cultural norms. Bolivia, Peru, and Ecuador, for example, have significant Indian populations who speak their own languages and follow their own customs. In Paraguay the main Indian language, Guaraní, is accepted as official along with Spanish. Nor are all South Americans Catholics. Today Protestantism is making steady gains, while in Brazil many citizens practice African religions right along with Catholicism and Protestantism.

South America is a lightly populated continent, having just 6 percent of the world's people. It is also the world's most tropical continent, for a larger percentage of its land falls between the tropics of Cancer and Capricorn than is the case with any other continent. The world's driest desert is there, the Atacama in northern Chile, where no one has ever seen a drop of rain fall. And the world's wettest place is there too, the Chocó region of Colombia, along that country's border with Panama. There it rains almost every day. South America also has some of the world's highest mountains, the Andes,

Volcanic scenery near Punta Espinosa on Fernandina, one of the Galápagos Islands.

and its greatest river, the Amazon.

So welcome to South America! Through this colorfully illustrated series of books you will travel through 12 countries, from giant Brazil to small Suriname. On your way you will learn about the geography, the history, the economy, and the people of each one. Geared to the needs of teachers and students, each volume contains book and web sources for further study, a chronology, project and report ideas, and even recipes of tasty and easy-to-prepare dishes popular in the countries studied. Each volume describes the country's national holidays and the cities and towns where they are held. And each book is indexed.

You are embarking on a voyage of discovery that will take you to lands not so far away, but as interesting and exotic as any in the world.

(Opposite) The sun sets over the rain forest along the Napo River, near the headwaters of the Amazon. (Right) Lago Cuicocha is a crater lake formed near a dormant volcano in the Cordillera Occidental. Islands in the lake are the remnants of lava domes from volcanic activity more than 3,000 years ago.

1 Big Things in Little Packages

ECUADOR IS THE smallest of the nations located on the western coast of South America. Bordered by Colombia, Peru, and the Pacific Ocean, Ecuador offers a breathtaking variety of landscapes. The majestic Andes Mountains run through the center of the country. Ecuador is also home to tropical rain forests, snow-capped volcanoes, glacier-fed lakes, *cloud forests*, tropical *savannas*, moist *mangrove* forests, and volcanic islands.

Ecuador is generally divided into four primary geographic regions. The Costa refers to the plain along Ecuador's coast. It covers about one-quarter of the nation's area. The Sierra is Ecuador's central highlands. Here, the Andes Mountains hem in a slender central *plateau*. The Oriente, a rain forest area east of the Andes, covers about one-half of the country. The last region is a famous *archipelago* called the Galápagos Islands. The Galápagos Islands are a group of about 15 large and hundreds of small islands. They were formed from volcanic lava and are composed mainly of a type of rock called basalt. They are home to more than 5,000 animal and plant species, including some of the world's most unusual creatures.

The Costa

The coastal region of Ecuador lies west of the great Andean range. It is a flat plain composed of three main types of ecosystems: tropical rain forests, tropical savannas, and dry forests.

Marine iguanas sun themselves on Isla Fernandina. The Galápagos Islands are considered a national treasure.

Ecuador's coast is dotted with resort towns, small fishing villages, parks, reserves, and deserted beaches. It is home to the world's largest remaining mangrove forest and to Ecuador's largest city, Guayaquil. The coast is also home to a large number of shrimp farms.

Shrimp farms are not the only farms found along Ecuador's coast. The rich soils of the Costa produce great crops of papaya, passion fruit, melon, watermelon, and mango. The Costa is also home to huge banana, coffee, *cacao*, African palm, and rice plantations.

The Sierra

The Sierra region is a narrow swath of lofty volcanoes and highland valleys. It lies between two chains of the Andes, the Cordillera Occidental (western) and the Cordillera Oriental (eastern). Together, these mountain ranges have more than a dozen peaks that tower over 16,000 feet (4,880 meters). Within the Sierra region, there are grassy highlands, called *páramos*, as well as cloud forests, mountain lakes, and active volcanoes.

Páramos, found between 11,480 and 14,750 feet (3,500 and 4,500 meters) above sea level, provide an excellent habitat for many of Ecuador's animals and plants. These include condors, llamas, multicolored flowers, and hummingbirds. The animals and plants of this region have adapted to low temperatures, strong winds, rain, hail, snow, and high **altitudes**.

Cloud forests support a large variety of plants and animals, from howler monkeys to gray-breasted mountain toucans. Cloud forests pull life-giving moisture from the thick cloud and fog banks that roll in off the ocean every year. During a fog season that lasts six months, two and a half acres (one

Quick Facts: The Geography of Ecuador

Location: Western South America, bordering the Pacific Ocean at the equator, between Colombia and Peru

Area[1]: (slightly smaller than Nevada)
total: 109,483 square miles (283,560 sq km)
land: 106,888 square miles (276,840 sq km)
water: 2,595 square miles (6,720 sq km)

Borders: Colombia, 367 miles (590 km); Peru, 882 miles (1,420 km)

Climate: tropical along coast, becoming cooler inland at higher elevations; tropical in Amazonian jungle lowlands

Terrain: coastal plain (Costa), inter-Andean central highlands (Sierra), and flat to rolling eastern jungle (Oriente)

Elevation extremes:
lowest point: Pacific Ocean—0 feet
highest point: Chimborazo—20,561 feet (6,267 meters)

Natural hazards: frequent earthquakes, landslides, volcanic activity; floods; periodic droughts

[1]includes Galápagos Islands.
Source: Adapted from CIA World Factbook 2002.

hectare) of cloud forest can trap about a million gallons (3.8 million liters) of water. This allows the forest to support itself during times of drought.

The western and eastern Andean ranges and their valley have been called the "Avenue of the Volcanoes." The most famous of these volcanoes are Chimborazo (20,696 feet/6,267 meters); Cotopaxi (19,614 feet/5,982 meters), the highest active volcano in the world; and Cayambe (18,992 feet/5,793 meters), a snow-capped volcano right on the equator. Twenty-two mountain peaks between 14,000 and 20,000 feet (4,270 and 6,100 meters) in altitude dominate the Andean ranges of the Sierra region.

The Oriente

Approximately 46,332 square miles (119,954 sq km) in area, the Oriente is bordered to the west by the Andes Mountains. Peru lies to its south and east and Colombia to its north. The Oriente's extensive rain forest covers about one-half of the country. It is part of South America's huge Amazon rain forest. The terrain of the Oriente is composed of gentle slopes and flat valleys. Many *tributaries* of the Amazon River run through the Oriente.

In certain sections of this jungle, more than 100 different species of trees have been recorded per acre. The Amazon region's rivers, lakes, streams, and marshlands support over 600 species of fish. More than 250 species of amphibians and reptiles can be found here as well.

Many mammals make their homes in Ecuador's Amazon rain forest,

Cotopaxi, the highest active volcano in the world, in the early morning. The area around Cotopaxi is a national park.

including armadillos, honey bears, and sloths. There are over 60 species of Amazon bats. Other mammals found in the tropical forest include tapirs, monkeys, and ocelots (or jaguars). The jungle's shallow ponds, or lagoons, support manatees and caimans, a kind of crocodile. Approximately 1,000 species of birds live in the Oriente's forest habitats, lagoons, and savannas. Parrots, macaws, and tanagers can be found among the trees. In the waterways, darters, herons, and gulls thrive.

To preserve these precious areas, Ecuador has created protected lands such as the Yasuni National Park Biosphere Reserve, the Limoncocha Ecological Reserve, and the Cuyabeno Wildlife Reserve. Ecuador's extensive national park system and protected areas include almost 8 million acres (3 million hectares). This helps to protect the endangered animals that live within these areas, such as the giant river otter and the howler monkey.

The Galápagos

Perhaps Ecuador's most famous region is the Galápagos Islands. These islands are approximately 600 miles (966 km) off the coast of Ecuador. They were formed by the eruption of volcanoes that are now extinct.

Covering an area of 12,798 square miles (33,134 sq km), the Galápagos region is an amazing place. There are about 10,000 people living on the Galápagos Islands, but the islands' most famous residents are plants and animals. There are over 5,000 species living on the Galápagos Islands. The islands are one of the most biologically *diverse* areas in the world. According to scientists, more than 1,900 of these species are found nowhere else. This is because the islands are so isolated. Over time, the plants and animals there developed characteristics different from those found anywhere else in the world.

The famous British naturalist Charles Darwin visited the Galápagos Islands in 1835. He used his studies of the unique animals there to develop his theory of evolution, publishing his ideas in *On the Origin of Species* in 1859.

Ecuador considers these islands a national treasure. Ninety-seven percent of the Galápagos Islands' land area is now a national park. Some of the islands' unique residents include Galápagos fur seals, Galápagos penguins, marine iguanas, pega-pega trees, lava lizards, and Galápagos tortoises.

Climate and Seasons

Ecuador is located right on the equator. (Its name means equator in Spanish.) But that doesn't mean every part of the country is always hot and humid. Temperatures within this country can range from 100°F (38°C) in some places to 55°F (13°C) in others. Elevation plays a key part in the temperature differences within the four major regions of Ecuador. Areas of higher elevation are cooler than low-lying regions.

The seasons in Ecuador are not determined by temperature. They are determined by amount of precipitation. The rainy season is called winter. The dry season is summer.

The Costa is generally hot and humid. It has an average annual temperature of 78°F (26°C). The Oriente is even warmer and moister than the Costa. Temperatures average just above 100°F (38°C) in this tropical zone. The annual precipitation is about 80 inches (200 centimeters). Both the Costa and the Oriente experience their rainy season, or winter, between May and December.

The Sierra stays fairly mild all year because of its high elevation. Temperatures range between 45° and 70°F (8–21°C) depending upon elevation. The rainy season in this region is from November to May.

Even though the Galápagos Islands are located along the equator, they are not unbearably hot. The average year-round temperature in this region is 85°F (30°C), which is considered subtropical, or just below tropical. This is partly because the temperature of the surrounding waters is often affected by a current from the South Pole known as the Peru, or Humboldt, Current. This polar current helps to cool the temperature of the air above the Galápagos Islands.

Another reason for the subtropical climate of the Galápagos Islands is ocean upwelling. Upwelling, which refers to the rise of deep water to the surface, is caused by ocean currents and winds. The water rising from the bottom of the ocean is colder than the surface water. In some areas, the water temperature can fall below 68°F (20°C). This water cools the Galápagos Islands' climate, too.

The Galápagos Islands, like the rest of Ecuador, have two seasons. The cold Humboldt Current brings what is known as the *garúa*. This is an ocean fog that influences the weather on the islands from July to December. A warmer current called El Niño shapes the weather on the islands from January to June. El Niño brings seasonal rain and slightly warmer weather with it.

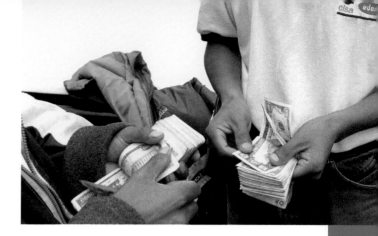

(Opposite) The Inca ruins of Ingapirca are located near Cuenca. They are the only Inca ruins in Ecuador. (Right) A man buys dollars from a street money changer in downtown Quito, January 2000. The "dollarization" plan was intended to stop rampant inflation that had led to the devaluation of the national currency of Ecuador.

2 Incas, Independence, and Oil

THE REGION THAT IS now Ecuador has been inhabited for at least 5,000 years. Archaeologists believe that at one time at least 50 different tribes of Native Americans lived along the coast, in the Sierra, and in the Amazon rain forest. These tribes were often at war. This left them vulnerable to conquest from outside groups. In the 15th century A.D., that is exactly what happened. The Ecuadorian tribes were conquered by the Inca, a powerful group of Native Americans from the highlands in present-day Peru. They added Ecuador to their huge empire.

The Incas ruled Ecuador for approximately 100 years. Their civilization was very advanced. They built great cities, temples, and pyramids through-out Ecuador. The height of their rule was in the late 15th century. At that point, the Incas controlled over 12 million people and 350,000 square miles (900,000 sq km) of land. They collected taxes, built roads and bridges, and practiced a formal religion. Their way of life came to an end after the 1530s when the Spanish, led by the famed *conquistador* Francisco Pizarro, conquered them. By 1572 the Incan Empire was completely destroyed.

The Colonial Period

After Pizarro conquered the Incas, Ecuador became a colony of Spain. It remained under Spanish rule for almost three centuries. Scholars, geographers, and mathematicians came to Ecuador to study and work in the New World. Two such men were Charles Marie de la Condamine, a French geographer and mathematician, and Alexander von Humboldt, a German geographer.

The Spanish set up large plantations and began growing a variety of crops. They forced the Native Americans to work on these plantations. They soon needed more workers and began importing black slaves from Africa to work the fields, too.

Around the turn of the 19th century, a *mestizo* named Eugenio Espejo was preaching revolution and independence. Espejo founded the country's first newspaper, *Primicias de la Cultura de Quito*. He is considered one of Ecuador's national heroes.

Espejo's ideas soon caught on. Other colonies in South America wanted independence from Spain, too. A Venezuelan leader, Simón Bolívar, successfully fought the Spanish and gained independence for Ecuador and other neighboring areas.

On July 24, 1822, a historic meeting between Bolívar and Argentinean rebel leader José de San Martín took place in Guayaquil. Bolívar convinced San Martín and other leaders to establish the Republic of Greater (Gran) Colombia. It included what are today Colombia, Ecuador, Venezuela, and Panama. Simón Bolívar was the republic's first president.

The Republic of Ecuador

The Republic of Greater Colombia did not last very long. The different regions soon began arguing. Ecuador pulled out of the republic and adopted its own constitution on September 23, 1830. This was also the year that Simón Bolívar died. He was only 47 years old. Ecuadorans mourned his death greatly.

The first years of the Republic of Ecuador were marked by power struggles and constant change. The first president was General Juan José Flores. He used the military to maintain his power. After he was overthrown in 1845, Ecuador experienced years of turmoil.

Simón Bolívar (1783–1830) is one of the most famous figures in South America's history. Under the general's leadership, Ecuador and other parts of South America were freed from Spanish control. Bolívar was the first president of the Republic of Greater Colombia, which included Ecuador from 1822 to 1830.

José María Urbina eventually became president in 1851. He was from the city of Guayaquil and represented business owners there who wanted to gain power at the expense of longtime landowners in the Sierra. These business owners formed a political group known as the Liberals. Urbina abolished slavery in 1852.

By 1859 Ecuador was almost falling apart. Some areas were in rebellion, and troops from Peru had invaded. In 1861 Gabriel García Moreno united the country and defeated the Peruvians. He would rule Ecuador for years. Moreno, who belonged to a political faction known as the Conservatives, favored the white ruling classes and increased the power of the Catholic Church. Although he was a *dictator*, Moreno improved education and transportation in Ecuador. He was assassinated in 1875.

In the last part of the 19th century, the country flourished economically.

Farmers hold up placards during a 1968 protest march in Quito. The farmers were angry about the death of rural workers at the hands of police.

This was mainly due to exports of cocoa, which is made from cacao beans. During this time, the government changed every few years. It continued to be unstable throughout the early 20th century. The Liberals and Conservatives were constantly fighting for power. Although some presidents were legally elected, others gained power through *coups d'etat*. During the 1920s and 1930s, life in Ecuador took a turn for the worse when the cocoa trade fell on hard times.

Modern Ecuador

After World War II, Ecuador's economy prospered as a result of a different crop: bananas. The country experienced a period of peace from 1948 to 1960. During this time, Ecuador's leaders were democratically elected. This period of stable democracy ended along with the banana boom in the early 1960s. A military *junta* led the country from 1963 to 1966. Presidential elections were held in 1968, and longtime politician José María Velasco Ibarra was elected for the fifth time. But by 1972, the commander-in-chief of the army, General Guillermo Rodríguez Lara, had removed Velasco from office.

The 1970s saw a return to economic prosperity. Ecuador became a major exporter of oil. Still, the government remained unstable. Other members of the military forced Rodríguez Lara to resign in 1976. Ecuador struggled to return to democracy.

The 1980s were hard years for Ecuador. The collapse of world oil prices in 1986 reduced Ecuador's oil export revenues tremendously. An earthquake in March 1987 wrecked a long section of Ecuador's oil pipeline. It seemed the economy and Mother Nature were working against Ecuador.

Throughout the 1990s, Ecuador suffered from corruption and incompetence in government. Sixto Duran, president from 1992 to 1996, lost the presidency after a corruption scandal. In 1996 Abdalá Bucaram was inaugurated. He spent only a short time in office. A general strike turned into a national protest in February 1997. It won the support of organized labor, business and professional organizations, and most of the Ecuadorian people. Congress declared Bucaram to be "loco," which means mentally unstable, and removed him from office.

Beginning in 1995, Ecuador began fighting with Peru over a border dispute dating back to colonial times. On October 26, 1998, the conflict finally ended when the president of Ecuador, Jamil Mahuad, and the president of Peru, Alberto Fujimori, signed the Peace Agreements of Brasília.

The economic situation in Ecuador grew dramatically worse in the late 1990s. Oil prices dropped. A particularly strong El Niño caused heavy rains and coastal flooding that killed nearly 200 people. To make matters worse, the national currency, the sucre, fell to an all-time low. On January 9, 2000, President Mahuad announced a radical plan to help the economy. He changed the legal currency of Ecuador from the sucre to the U.S. dollar, a process he called "dollarization." Over a six-month transition period, Ecuadorans traded in their sucres for U.S. dollars at a rate of 25,000 sucres per dollar.

The "dollarization" program angered many people, as did corruption in Mahuad's administration. On January 21, 2000, indigenous Ecuadorans, supported by the military, forced Mahuad out of office. Vice President Gustavo Bejarano Noboa was sworn in as president.

In September 2001, Luis Maldonado was sworn in as minister of social welfare. Maldonado became the first Ecuadorian Indian to hold a cabinet post not dealing solely with the affairs of native people.

Ecuador was forced to declare a national emergency in March 2002. Winter storms raged for over a month, dumping heavy rains upon the nation. Thirteen people were killed and the storms caused millions of dollars in property damage.

The early twenty-first century proved a highly turbulent time for Ecuadorian politics. In 2002, voters elected Lucio Gutiérrez, a former army colonel, to be president. Ecuadorians hoped he would fight corruption as he'd promised, but his government was often accused of political misdeeds. After he dismissed the Supreme Court and imposed a state of emergency in Quito in 2005, Congress removed him from office amidst nationwide fears that he would become a dictator. His replacement, former vice-president Alfredo Palacio, focused on amending the Constitution and lowering inflation. Palacio left office with fairly high approval ratings in 2007, when newly elected president Rafael Correa was sworn in. A sharp critic of the United States and an advocate of social change, Correa became Ecuador's eighth president in ten years.

Gustavo Bejarano Noboa became president in 2000, after a coup toppled unpopular president Jamil Mahuad from office.

(Opposite) Farmers work in a field in the highlands. About 7 percent of Ecuador's workforce is employed in agriculture. (Right) A man walks with his dogs along a pipeline that brings oil from the Amazon Basin to the west coast of Ecuador. Oil remains an important part of the country's economy.

3 The Economy of Ecuador

FOR MANY YEARS, Ecuador's primary export was bananas. That changed with the discovery of oil in the early 1970s. The oil industry brought a lot of money into Ecuador very quickly. By the 1980s, half of Ecuador's export earnings came from oil.

Unfortunately, oil has not solved Ecuador's economic problems. The second half of the 1990s was very difficult for Ecuador. The nation sank into its worst depression in almost 100 years. It was forced to abandon its own currency, the sucre, and adopt the U.S. dollar. Still, almost half of the government's revenue comes from the oil industry. The government has high hopes that the oil industry will improve once more and help save Ecuador's faltering economy.

Not all Ecuadorians agree that oil is good for Ecuador. Native people are suing oil companies for damage done by oil spills and other oil-related pollution to their rivers, forests, animals, and families.

Banana Trading Houses

About one-third of Ecuador's bananas are shipped to the United States. Countries like Russia, Japan, and others import the rest of Ecuador's large banana crops. Noboa, the national Ecuadorian banana producer, is the fourth-largest banana company in the world.

Most banana farms in Ecuador are about 100 to 150 acres (40 to 60 hectares) in size. These farms sell their bananas to large banana trading houses that distribute the fruit throughout the world. Almost 10 percent of

Workers wash and weigh green bananas at a Dole processing plant near Guayaquil. Bananas have been a major export crop in Ecuador since the 19th century.

A flower vendor sells a bouquet to a young man from a stand on a street in Quito. Flower cultivation—particularly roses—has become a big business in Ecuador. More than 70 percent of Ecuador's flower exports go to the United States.

Ecuador's population works for the banana industry.

Banana workers in Ecuador are paid very poorly. They receive few, if any, benefits such as health care or paid vacation time. In 1999 their average wages were less than $60 a month. In Panama, a nearby Central American country, workers doing the same jobs were making $500 a month.

Shrimp and Flowers

After bananas, shrimp is Ecuador's largest export food product. Ecuador is the largest producer of farmed shrimp in Latin America. It is the fourth-largest producer in the world.

Unfortunately, shrimp farms destroy mangrove forests. Shrimp farmers clear the forests to make way for special ponds used to raise shrimp. Sixty-five percent of Ecuador's mangrove forest destruction can be linked directly to shrimp farms. Although the typical small shrimp farm may earn anywhere from $1,500 to $5,000 a year for its owner, the environment pays a high price. Mangrove trees provide an ecosystem for many kinds of fish and other marine life. Without the mangroves, the fish die. Ecuadorians are beginning to look into ways to reduce the environmental impact of shrimp farms.

Flower production has become a major part of Ecuador's economy. More than a billion roses are grown in the country every year! Flowers are farmed throughout the Sierra on large plantations. Ecuadorian women make up over 70 percent of the workforce for the flower industry. Most of these women have jobs growing and harvesting the flowers. Men who work in the flower industry are generally hired to perform heavy labor. Most work in maintenance positions, water the flowers, or spray them to control bugs.

Compared with banana workers, flower workers are very well paid. In 1997 Ecuadoran flower workers were making close to $200 a month. This makes a job on a flower plantation a very desirable position for a young rural worker.

Unemployment and Poverty

In 2006 approximately 38 percent of Ecuadorans were living below the poverty line. Although the Ecuadorian unemployment rate—estimated at 9% in 2007—has dropped in recent years from much higher totals, *underemployment* remains widespread. The rural areas of Ecuador have a higher poverty level than do the urban areas, but poverty is found throughout the country.

Quick Facts: The Economy of Ecuador

Gross domestic product (GDP*):
$98.79 billion (purchasing power parity)

GDP per capita: $7,200

Inflation: 2.2%

Natural resources: petroleum, fish, timber, hydropower

Agriculture (6.7% of GDP): bananas, coffee, cocoa, rice, potatoes, manioc (tapioca), plantains, sugarcane; cattle, sheep, pigs, beef, pork, dairy products; balsa wood; fish, shrimp

Industry (35.1% of GDP): petroleum, food processing, textiles, wood products, chemicals

Services (58.2% of GDP): government, banking, tourism

Foreign trade:

Exports—$14.37 billion: petroleum, bananas, cut flowers, shrimp, cacao, coffee, hemp, wood, fish

Imports—$12.76 billion: industrial materials, fuels and lubricants, non-durable consumer goods

Currency exchange rate: U.S. dollar is official currency.

* GDP or gross domestic product = the total value of goods and services produced in a year.
Sources: World Bank; CIA World Factbook 2008.
All figures are 2007 estimates unless otherwise noted.

Ecuadorans try to make a living any way they can. Street vendors called *ambulantes* roam city streets peddling their wares. Some sell food they have cooked at home. Others sell items they have bought cheaply, made, or stolen. Almost all are simply trying to make enough money to feed themselves and their families.

Ecuador's economic hopes for the future are based primarily upon the dollarization program and increased oil exploration and production. Still, the tiny nation has room to expand in other industries, too. The increasing

Native Americans in Ecuador sell a variety of items at the Saquisili market.

demand for Ecuadorian flowers should continue to help the nation's economy. A carefully supervised lumber industry could help increase the nation's revenue flow. Better-managed shrimp farms and continued banana sales will contribute to the nation's economic stabilization.

By many indicators, the economy of Ecuador has improved in recent years, and the quality of life with it. In 2006, 38% of Ecuadorians were estimated to live below the poverty line, and 9% were unemployed in 2007—compared to 2001, when 70% lived in poverty and 14% were unemployed. As the country adjusted to new economic policies such as dollarization, the inflation rate fell dramatically, and goods and services produced more money. Under President Rafael Correa, Ecuador managed to pay off outstanding debt. Still, living conditions are very difficult for large numbers of citizens, and many of those who have jobs are forced to work in unsafe conditions for low pay. The future of the Ecuadorian petroleum industry is uncertain, since production has dropped as demand increases. While the Ecuadorian economy is growing, it remains fragile.

(Opposite) A small cottage with a thatched roof in the highlands of Ecuador, near Saquisili. Many Otavaleño Indians still live in the area. The Otavaleño are one of the tribes indigenous to the region. (Right) A woman cooks a guinea pig over an open fire. This traditional meal has been enjoyed in Ecuador since before the Incas arrived.

4 From Shamans to Cyber Cafés

ONE-FOURTH OF ECUADOR'S population is Native American, or Amerindian. The largest Amerindian group is the Quichua, native to the Andes Mountains. This group numbers more than 2 million. In addition to the Quichua, the Otavaleños, Salasacas, and Saraguros also live in the Andes. These Indian peoples still speak the ancient language of the Incas, Quechua. Deep in the Amazon Basin live the Huaorani, Zaparo, Cofán, lowland Quichua, Siona, Secoya, Shuar, and Achuar. These people still keep to the old ways of their ancestors. Some groups still speak their own languages.

Many of Ecuador's native people are shepherds. Others are small farmers and cattle ranchers. More and more are beginning to sell cloth goods that they weave themselves.

Quick Facts: The People of Ecuador

Population: 13,927,650

Ethnic groups: mestizo (mixed Amerindian and white), 65%; Amerindian, 25%; Spanish and others, 7%; black, 3%

Age structure:
0–14 years: 32.1%
15–64 years: 62.7%
65 years and over: 5.2%

Population growth rate: 0.94%

Birth rate: 21.54 births/1,000 population

Death rate: 4.21 deaths/1,000 population

Infant mortality rate: 21.35 deaths / 1,000 live births

Life expectancy at birth:
total population: 76.81 years
male: 73.94 years
female: 79.84 years

Total fertility rate: 2.59 children born per woman

Religions: Roman Catholic, 95%

Languages: Spanish (official), Amerindian languages (especially Quechua)

Literacy rate (age 15 and older): 91% (2001 est.)

Source: CIA World Factbook 2008. All figures are 2008 estimates unless otherwise noted.

In addition to the numerous native cultures, Ecuador is home to a mestizo culture. Ecuador's mestizos are descended from native people and Spanish settlers.

Ecuador also has an Afro-Ecuadorian culture. Approximately 3 percent of Ecuador's population is black. These people are the descendants of African slaves. Many of their ancestors worked on sugar plantations during the colonial days of Ecuador. Once freed from slavery, many stayed in Ecuador and created new lives for themselves and their children.

White, black, and mestizo Ecuadorians speak Spanish. Spanish is Ecuador's official language.

Ecuador has an informal social class structure left over from colonial times. Whites tend to be among the wealthy upper classes, with Indians and blacks at the bottom of the social ladder. There is a large gap between the rich upper class of Ecuador and the poor, lower class. The middle class that separated the two for many years seems to be almost disappearing. During Ecuador's decades of financial instability, its richest citizens gained new wealth while everyone else grew poorer.

Chimbacucho, a small village in Ecuador, is home to a group of Quichua Indians, the Tigua. The Tigua are becoming famous for paintings that depict scenes and events from their daily lives. The paintings are done using oil, acrylic, or enamel paints on sheep hide.

The first Tigua artist to become well known for such paintings was a man named Julio Toaquiza. He was a poor farmer who at first sold drums and masks that he painted. An art dealer from the capital city of Quito suggested that he try his hand at painting on sheep's hide. Toaquiza became quite skilled at this new art style. He now trains people from Chimbacucho to paint on sheep's hides as well, and art collectors are taking notice.

A unique instrument, called the *coroneta*, is made from cow horns. Cowhide is also used on this traditional drum. Ecuadorian music is enjoyed throughout the world.

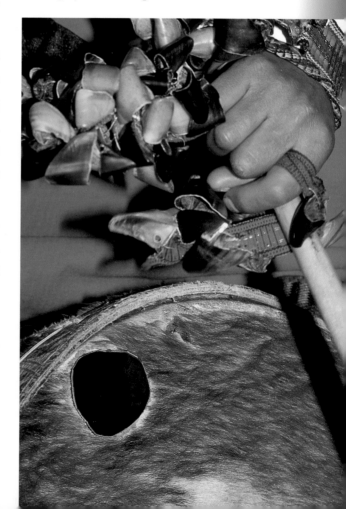

Ecuador also boasts a number of internationally known painters. Oswaldo Guayasamin (1919–1999) is the most famous. His work won many awards and was exhibited all over the world.

Music

Andean, African, and European music have combined in Ecuador to create a music that is known throughout the world. It is called *bomba* after the type of Ecuadorian drum used to keep the beat.

Many of the blacks who live in the province of Esmeraldas enjoy a special music called marimba. Marimba music is a traditional African music. According to African legends, a princess named Marimba created the first marimba, an instrument like a xylophone, but made of wood. She named it after herself. When the princess died, she became the goddess of music. The music people made using the marimba came to be named for the princess as well. In Ecuador, marimba music is played at funerals, festivals, and celebrations. It has spread throughout Latin America.

Another popular form of music in

A smiling Ecuadorian girl. Most of Ecuador's 14 million people are mestizos—of mixed Amerindian and white heritage.

A priest delivers Communion in an ornate Roman Catholic church in Quito. Nearly all of Ecuador's people are Roman Catholic.

Ecuador is a type of folk music called *pasillo*. It is based on the traditional European waltz but features sad melodies and words.

Sports and Entertainment

The most popular sport in Ecuador is soccer, called *fútbol*. Ecuadorians love to go to stadiums to cheer on their favorite team. In 2002 Ecuadorans were very proud of their national soccer team. It qualified for the international

World Cup tournament for the first time in Ecuador's history, making the first round. Since then, the team has qualified again, finishing in the second round during the 2006 World Cup.

Dancing is one of Ecuador's favorite forms of entertainment. Ecuadorians dance at festivals, weddings, parties, and other celebrations. Neighborhood parties are often held in the village streets. During these, Ecuadorians of all ages dance together. In cities like Quito and Guayaquil, Ecuadorians dance to popular Latin and American music in disco clubs.

Education and Religion

Children in Ecuador must attend school for at least eight years. They go to kindergarten for two years and then to elementary school for six years. After that, they may attend secondary school. After completing secondary school, students receive diplomas.

Ecuadorans have a great love for children. When a woman is pregnant, they refer to the baby she is carrying as a *luz* ("light"). Often, people will stop a pregnant woman and ask her when her new "light" will arrive.

The major religion in Ecuador is Roman Catholicism. The Spanish who colonized Ecuador brought this religion with them. Spanish missionaries started some of Ecuador's first schools. However, the native people of Ecuador mix elements of their older, *pre-Columbian* religions with Catholicism.

Shamans are an important part of some of these old religions. A shaman is like a combination of holy man and doctor. Some native people believe their shamans can heal through magic or through power from the tribe's gods. Shamans who still practice ancient traditions are very knowledgeable about the healing qualities of natural substances. Many use plants and herbs to create medicines for the people of their villages.

Cyber Cafés

A 2006 survey reported that there were more than 1.5 million Internet users in this small nation. As not all Ecuadorians can afford their own computers, Internet cafés are becoming more and more common in Ecuador's larger cities. Ecuadorians gather in these cafés to share conversation, surf the Internet, and indulge in a cup of coffee or a bite to eat.

(Opposite) Downtown Quito, Ecuador's capital and second-largest city. (Right) Guayaquil is Ecuador's largest city, with a population of 1.6 million. Many of its poor residents live in slums such as this one at Isla Trinitario.

5 Cities and Communities

ECUADOR IS DIVIDED into 24 provinces. Each of these provinces is subdivided into regions. The regions are divided into parishes, which are sometimes divided into even smaller *caserios*, or villages. The 24 provinces of Ecuador are Azuay, Bolívar, Canar, Carchi, Chimborazo, Cotopaxi, El Oro, Esmeraldas, Galápagos, Guayas, Imbabura, Loja, Los Rios, Manabi, Morona-Santiago, Napo, Orellana, Pastaza, Pichincha, Santa Elena, Santo Domingo de los Tsachilas, Sucumbios, Tungurahua, and Zamora-Chinchipe.

Guayaquil

The largest city in Ecuador is Guayaquil, with a population of approximatley 1.6 million. Established by the Spanish in its present location in 1537, it sits on the Guayas River about 40 miles (64 km) from the coast. Today it is Ecuador's main port.

Guayaquil got its name in a rather tragic way. According to legend, the chief of the Puna Indians, Guayas, fought bravely against the invading Spaniards. When it became clear that he would be defeated, Guayas made a desperate decision. He killed his wife, Quila, then drowned himself. He did this to prevent the Spaniards from capturing his wife or himself. Guayaquil is a combination of both of their names.

Guayaquil has an interesting history. During colonial times it was frequently attacked by pirates. Fires destroyed large parts of the city during the 18th and 19th centuries. And in 1822, Guayaquil served as the meeting place of two of South America's most famous independence fighters: Simón Bolívar and José de San Martín.

Today the city, in addition to serving as Ecuador's main port, is an industrial center. Its businesses include tanneries, iron foundries, and sugar refineries.

Tourist attractions include a 16th-century church. Also popular is the Botanical Garden in Guayaquil, home to one of the world's finest displays of orchids. There are usually at least 50 different species of orchids on display. The Botanical Garden also boasts a fine collection of more than 320 different species of other plants. Fluttering wings are another beautiful aspect of Guayaquil's Botanical Garden. Over 60 types of butterflies amaze and delight visitors. There are also over 70 species of birds on display.

Quito

Quito, the second-largest Ecuadoran city, is home to about 1.18 million people. Located in the Sierra, it is the capital of Ecuador.

Panecillo Hill and the Winged Virgin statue, at the left in this photograph of Quito, provide a spectacular view of the old and new areas of the city, as well as the surrounding mountains.

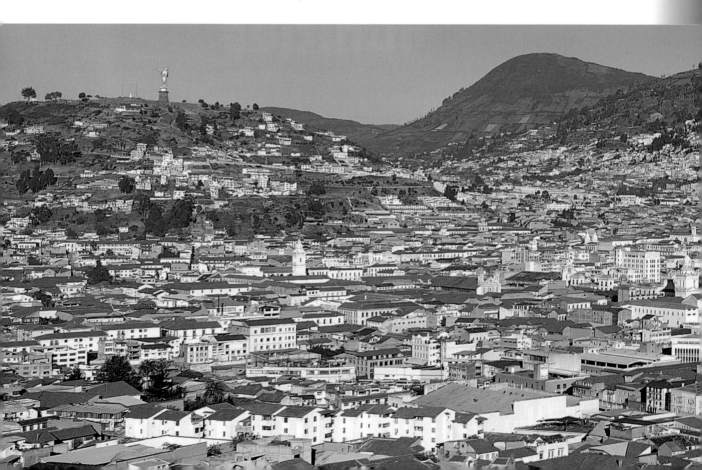

People have been living in the Quito area for more than 2,000 years! In 1487 the Incas captured the city. They made it the capital of the northern part of their empire. The Incas destroyed the city in the 16th century so the Spanish could not capture it. The Spanish quickly rebuilt Quito, and it became an important colonial city.

Just north of Quito is a statue that was built to mark the equator. Here visitors find a large stone monument topped by a brass globe. The name of this monument is La Mitad del Mundo, or the middle of the world. The equator is also marked by a small concrete sphere that rests to the south of Cayambe, not far from the village of Guayllabamba.

Quito has two main sections: Old Town, where Spanish colonial buildings remain, and New Town. Old Town is filled with colonial plazas and churches. The famous Plaza de la Independencia is located here. This was the center of the Spanish colonial city of Quito. It is decorated with flowers, fountains, and palm trees.

New Town is Quito's modern section. It features new hotels, shops, and restaurants. There are also museums filled with art and archaeological artifacts. Museum entrance fees are very low compared with American prices. Some are as low as 50 cents.

One of New Town's famous museums is the Museo Guayasamin. The museum has permanent and changing collections of modern Ecuadoran art on display. It was named in honor of the Ecuadoran artist Oswaldo Guayasamin. Much of his work is now housed at this museum.

Also, the Museo del Banco Central is located in Quito. This museum exhibits Incan and Canari artifacts. With examples of Incan pottery, a mummy, and Spanish colonial furniture, this is easily the best archaeology museum in all of Ecuador.

North of Quito are 15 pyramids. Scholars believe they were built by the Cara Indians. These pyramids are called the pyramids of Cochasqui. There are also more than 20 funeral or burial mounds at the site. Indians and other local Ecuadorans visit this area during *solstices* and *equinoxes*. During these times, people celebrate and honor the passage of the sun. Shamans bless the people and their crops with rituals that date back to Ecuador's pre-Inca history. Like their ancestors before them, most of these Indians see the sun as the source of all life.

Otavalo

About 42 miles (68 km) north of Quito is another of the Sierra's important communities, Otavalo. Otavalo is famous for its open-air market. The craft market is centered in and around the Plaza de Los Ponchos at the northeastern edge of the city. The market is known throughout Latin America for its colorful, handmade sweaters and crafts. Otavalo is a popular tourist destination.

The town was originally a settlement of the Otavalo Indians. The Spanish occupied it in the 16th century. In 1868 a large earthquake devastated Otavalo, but it was later rebuilt.

Cuenca

Cuenca, located about 68 miles (109 km) southeast of Guayaquil, is not nearly as large as Quito or Guayaquil. Still, with over 200,000 people, it is

Ecuador's third-largest city. It is the capital of Azuay province.

In 1557 the Spanish founded Cuenca on the site of an Amerindian village called Tumibamba. Much of Cuenca's architecture dates from the Spanish colonial period. The city's whitewashed buildings, red-tiled roofs, cobblestone streets, and public plazas add to its Old World atmosphere. Today, the city of Cuenca is considered one of the centers of Ecuadorian culture. It has long been home to some of Ecuador's leading writers, artists, and *intellectuals*.

Ecuador's best religious museum is in Cuenca. It is called the Museo de las Conceptas. The museum is in a Catholic convent, the Convent of the

The view at dusk from El Panecillo, a hill that overlooks the whole of Quito.

Immaculate Conception. For one dollar, visitors can tour the building and view its collection. Part of the building, the infirmary, dates to 1599. There is also a display of crosses that were carved by the Ecuadoran sculptor Gaspar Sangurima.

Only 40 miles (64 km) from Cuenca stands the largest remaining Ecuadoran Incan structure, called the Ingapirca. Archaeologists believe that it once housed a temple built to honor the Incan sun god. They also believe that a part of the Ingapirca ruins was probably used as a *tambo*—a resting place for Incan messengers, or couriers. The Incas' system of roads and runners enabled official communications to travel from one end of their vast empire to the other with surprising speed. Couriers who stopped to rest at Ingapirca were most likely traveling the road to and from Quito.

A Calendar of Ecuadorian Festivals

January

On January 1 Ecuadorians celebrate the **New Year (Año Nuevo)** by burning a life-size dummy called the Año Viejo (Old Year). This ceremony symbolizes leaving the old year behind.

February

Carnaval is a huge celebration that takes place before **Ash Wednesday**. Ash Wednesday is the beginning of the Catholic period of **Lent**; the date changes from year to year, occuring either in February or in March. Carnaval parties can last for days or even weeks. There are water fights and parades throughout Ecuador.

April

Semana Santa, or Holy Week, is the week leading up to **Easter** (which usually occurs in March or April). It features many religious processions. Ecuadorians eat a traditional soup called *fanesca*, made with grain and codfish.

May

Labor Day celebrations, on May 1, feature parades honoring workers.

On May 24, the **anniversary of the 1822 Battle of Pichincha**, when Simón Bolívar's forces defeated the Spanish, is celebrated.

July

The **birthday of Simón Bolívar** is celebrated in all of Ecuador on July 24.

Residents celebrate the 1547 **Founding of Guayaquil** by Francisco de Orellana on July 25.

August

On August 10, the people of Ecuador celebrate **Independence Day**, recalling the day in 1822 when Ecuador won its freedon from Spain.

September

During the first two weeks of the month, the **Fiesta del Yamor** takes place in Otavalo. This festival features processions, music, dancing, fireworks, and the crowning of the Reina (Queen) de la Fiesta.

October

October 12 is **Día de la Raza** (Race Day) or **Columbus Day**. This holiday celebrates the Hispanic people of the world and Columbus's arrival in the New World.

November

November 2 is **Día de los Difuntos** (Day of the Dead), also called All Soul's Day. Ecuadorans pay their respects to the dead by visiting cemeteries and making bread people, or "guaguas de pan." They also make a blackberry drink called "colada morada."

The **Independence of Cuenca** was declared on November 3, and this is the last day of a large three-day celebration in the Andean city.

A Calendar of Ecuadorian Festivals

December

A celebration of the **Founding of Quito** is held December 6. The city holds world-famous bullfights on this anniversary of the founding of the present city by the Spanish.

In Ecuador **Christmas Day**, December 25, is spent with family. There is usually a feast in the evening. Gifts are opened after the feast.

Recipes

SALADS AND VINAIGRETTE

Vinaigrette
(Makes enough for 1 salad)
1 tbsp olive or vegetable oil
2 tbsp lemon juice
3 tbsp low-sodium chicken broth (skim fat)
1 tbsp Dijon mustard

Directions:
1. Mix together and use as salad dressing.

Lettuce and Potato Salad
2 cups chopped lettuce
2 cups cooked, peeled, diced potatoes
1 cup cooked green beans, cut into inch-long
   pieces
1 cup cooked peas
1 large tomato, diced
1 hard-boiled egg, sliced

Directions:
1. In a large bowl, mix the lettuce, potatoes, green
   beans, peas, and tomatoes.
2. Add the vinaigrette and toss.
3. Garnish with slices of hard-boiled egg and serve.

Red Pepper and Garbanzo Bean Salad
1 medium red bell pepper, diced
1 cup cooked garbanzo beans
1 1/2 cups chopped celery
1 small red onion, sliced
1 medium cucumber, thinly sliced

Directions:
1. In a large bowl, stir together all ingredients.
2. Add the vinaigrette and toss.
3. Cover and refrigerate for 30 minutes. Toss before
   serving.

Garden Salad with Mushrooms
1 cup cooked corn kernels
1 cup cooked, sliced carrots
1 cup cooked green beans
1 cup cooked peas
1 cup mushrooms

Directions:
1. In a large bowl, mix together all ingredients.
2. Add vinaigrette and toss.
3. Cover and refrigerate for 30 minutes. Toss before
   serving.

SOUPS

Locro
(Serves 4)
Kernels from 6 fresh ears of corn
3 tomatoes
1 onion
1 red pepper
2 garlic cloves, crushed
Olive oil
Water
1 slice sweet pumpkin, cubed
Salt to taste

Directions:
1. Chop tomatoes, onion, and pepper.
2. Sauté the onion, pepper, and garlic cloves in the oil until the onion is translucent.
3. Add tomatoes and the corn to the saucepan.
4. Add enough water to cover the mixture.
5. Bring to a boil.
6. Next, add pumpkin and salt to taste.
7. Lower the heat and simmer until the pumpkin is done.

Tomato Soup with Bananas
(Serves 4)
8 medium tomatoes, peeled and chopped
2 cups chicken stock
1/2 tsp salt
2 tbsp vegetable oil
2 onions, diced
4 bananas
1/8 tsp white pepper
1/4 cup half-and-half
2 tbsp cornstarch
2 tbsp coconut, grated

Directions:
1. In a large saucepan, combine tomatoes, stock, and salt. Bring to a boil, then cover and simmer over low heat. Let cook until tomatoes are soft.
2. Heat the oil in a saucepan. Add onions and sauté until transparent. Peel, then slice bananas. Add banana slices to sautéed onions. Sauté, mashing gently. Puree tomato pulp. Stir puree into onion mixture.
3. In separate mixing bowl, combine cornstarch and half-and-half. Stir in about 1/4 cup of the hot tomato soup. Stir cornstarch mixture into the rest of the soup. Stir constantly over low heat until soup thickens slightly. Season with white pepper. Garnish soup with coconut.

Glossary

altitude—height above sea level.

archipelago—a group of islands.

cacao—a bean used to make chocolate and cocoa.

cloud forest—a type of tropical forest that grows at high elevations and is often covered by clouds.

conquistador—a leader of the Spanish forces that conquered Central and South America in the 16th century.

coup d'etat—the sudden overthrow of a government, usually by violence.

dictator—a leader of a country who rules with absolute power and suppresses political opponents.

diverse—having great variety.

equinox—either of the two days each year (one in early spring, one in early fall) when the sun is above the equator, making the day and night equal in length throughout the world.

intellectual—a person who spends much of his or her time in study and research in an effort to increase society's knowledge.

junta—a small group of people that controls a government after seizing power.

mangrove—a type of tropical, coastal tree with long, exposed, tangled roots.

mestizo—a person of mixed Native American and white heritage.

plateau—a flat area of land at high elevation.

Glossary

pre-Columbian—characteristic of Amerindian cultures before the arrival of Christoper Columbus in 1492.

savanna—a flat area of land with large expanses of long, tough grass and occasional clumps of small trees.

solstice—either of the two days each year (one in early summer, one in early winter) when the sun is farthest from the equator, creating either the longest or shortest day of the year.

tributary—a stream or river that flows into a larger stream or river.

underemployment—employment that pays very poorly or is only part-time.

Project and Report Ideas

Literature

With help from your teacher or another adult, find and read the English translation of *The Victory at Junin: Song to Bolívar* by José Joaquín Olmedo (1780–1847). Write your own poem about a hero that you admire. Share your work with your class.

Math

Find out more about the sucre. How many sucres were exchanged for a dollar? What percentage of a dollar was a sucre? Why did Ecuador change its currency from sucres to dollars?

Science

Research the animals of the Galápagos Islands and Ecuador. Choose one insect, one mammal, one reptile, one fish, and one bird. Explain to your class what makes each of these animals special or unique.

Research the Galápagos Islands. How did the animals get there? Why are some of them unique to this region? What did Charles Darwin say about the animals of the Galápagos? Write a one-page report about your research and share it with your class.

History

Research the class structure of the ancient Incans. Compare and contrast Incan society to Spanish colonial society.

Who was Charles-Marie de la Condamine? What contribution did he make to the history of Ecuador? What was his most famous achievement?

Project and Report Ideas

Geography

Create a travel plan for a trip to Ecuador. Using maps of Ecuador, a travel book such as *The Lonely Planet Guide to Ecuador*, and this book, choose five places you would like to visit in Ecuador. Create a map showing the path your journey will take. Write a brief description of each stop along your trip. Describe the similarities and differences in the weather, terrain, and plant and animal life at each location you visit.

Art

Find examples of the art of Manuel Rendon, Eduardo Kingman, Juan Agustín Guerrero, and Oswaldo Guayasamin. Use the Internet and books for your research. Choose your favorite artist and artwork. Show some of the art to your classmates and tell them about the artist's life.

Find a recipe for *masapan* and make a bread dough doll. Explain to your classmates and teacher the importance of bread dough dolls in Ecuador. Teach your class how to make a bread dough doll.

Music

Research the flutes played by native people from Ecuador. Share what you learn with your class.

Have a dance that features only music from Ecuador. See if you can learn to dance to salsa!

Chronology

1450s	Incas of Peru conquer the Caras people.
1531	Spanish led by Francisco Pizarro land on Ecuadoran coast.
1534	Spanish conquer Ecuador.
1809	Ecuadorans begin calling for independence.
1822	Ecuador becomes part of independent Gran Colombia, with Colombia, Panama, and Venezuela.
1830	Ecuador leaves Gran Colombia, becoming an independent nation.
1941	Peru invades mineral-rich province of El Oro.
1942	Ecuador loses El Oro Province to Peru in agreement called the Rio Protocol.
1948–60	Banana trade improves economy.
1963	President Carlos Arosemena Monroy deposed. Military junta begins social and economic reforms.
1968	Former president José María Velasco elected president for the fifth time.
1972	Oil production starts.
1979	New constitution returns Ecuador to democracy.
1981	Border war with Peru erupts.
1982	Falling oil prices lead to economic depression, strikes, demonstrations, and a general state of emergency.
1987	President León Febres Cordero kidnapped and beaten up by the army.

1992	Native peoples granted title to 2.5 million acres (1 million hectares) in the Oriente.
1996	Abdalá Bucaram Ortíz elected president.
1997	Fabian Alarcón becomes president.
1998	Jamil Mahuad Witt elected president.
2000	Ecuador adopts the U.S. dollar as its national currency.
2001	In January, Ecuador declares state of emergency in Galápagos Islands after a cargo ship suffers a fuel spill. In September, Luis Maldonado is sworn in as minister of social welfare. He is the first Indian to hold a cabinet post that does not deal solely with the affairs of native people.
2002	Ecuador declares a national emergency due to damage and deaths caused by winter storms; Lucio Gutiérrez elected president in November.
2004	Ecuador celebrates 25 years of civilian government.
2005	Alfredo Palacio becomes president when Gutiérrez is removed from office after civil unrest.
2006	Rafael Correa is elected president, pledging to create economic and social changes for Ecuador, especially for the poor.
2008	Correa proposes a new constitution, to a mixed response from the nation; Ecuador re-establishes diplomacy with neighboring Colombia.

Further Reading/Internet Resources

Behnke, Alison. *Ecuador in Pictures*. Minneapolis: Lerner Publications, 2009.

Crowder, Nicholas. *Ecuador: A Survival Guide to Customs and Etiquette*. Tarrytown, N.Y.: Marshall Cavendish, 2007.

Kras, Sara Louise. *The Galápagos Islands*. New York: Benchmark Books, September 2008.

Palmerlee, Danny, et al. *Ecuador and the Galápagos Islands*. Oakland, Calif.: Lonely Planet, 2006.

de la Torre, Carlos, and Steve Striffler. *Ecuador Reader: History, Culture, Politics*. Durham, N.C.: Duke University Press, 2009.

History and Geography

http://geography.about.com/library/maps/blecuador.htm
http://memory.loc.gov/frd/cs/ectoc.html
http://www.travelforkids.com/Funtodo/Ecuador/ecuador.htm
http://www.flags.net/country.php?country=ECUA&section=CURR

Culture and Festivals

http://gosouthamerica.about.com/library/blEcuhol.htm
http://www.ecuadorexplorer.com/html/holidays.html
http://www.ecuador-travel-guide.org/thingstodo/Fest.htm

For More Information

Ecuadoran Embassy in Washington, D.C.
2535 15th St. NW
Washington, DC 20009
Telephone: (202) 234-7200
http://www.ecuador.org

Ecuadorian-American Chamber of Commerce - Guayaquil
G. Cordova 812, Piso 3, Oficina 1
Edificio Torres de la Merced
Guayaquil, Ecuador
Telephone: (593 4) 566-481 or 565-761
E-Mail: caecam1@caecam.org.ec
(Branch: Manchala)

Ecuadorian-American Chamber of Commerce - Quito
Ecuadorian American Chambers of Commerce
Av. 6 de Diciembre y La Niña
Multicentro - Floor 4
Quito - Ecuador
Telephone: (593 2) 250-7450
Fax: (593 2) 250-4571
E-mail: info@ecamcham.com

American Embassy in Quito
Avenida 12 de Octubre y Avenida Patria
Quito, Ecuador
Mailing address: APO AA 34039
Telephone: [593] (2) 256-2890
http://www.usembassy.org.ec/English/IndexEN.htm

Index

Index/Picture Credits

Page	
2:	© OTTN Publishing
3:	© OTTN Publishing
7:	Digital Vision, Ltd.
8:	Carl & Ann Purcell/Corbis
9:	Dan Heller Photography
10–11:	Digital Vision, Ltd.
14:	Digital Vision, Ltd.
18:	Pablo Corral Vega/Corbis
19:	AFP/Corbis
21:	Giraudon/Art Resource, NY
22:	Bettmann/Corbis
25:	Susana Gonzalez/Newsmakers/Getty Images
26:	Dan Heller Photography
27:	Justin Ide/Liaison/Getty Images
28:	Owen Franken/Corbis
29:	Pablo Corral Vega/Corbis
32:	Dan Heller Photography
34:	Dan Heller Photography
35:	Dan Heller Photography
37:	Jan Butchofsky-Houser/Houserstock
38:	Dan Heller Photography
39:	Owen Franken/Corbis
42:	Digital Vision, Ltd.
43:	Jeremy Horner/Corbis
45:	Digital Vision, Ltd.
48–49:	Digital Vision, Ltd.

Cover photo: (front) Used under license from Shutterstock, Inc.

Contributors

Senior Consulting Editor **James D. Henderson** is professor of international studies at Coastal Carolina University. He is the author of *Conservative Thought in Twentieth Century Latin America: The Ideals of Laureano Gómez* (1988; Spanish edition *Las ideas de Laureano Gómez* published in 1985); *When Colombia Bled: A History of the Violence in Tolima* (1985; Spanish edition *Cuando Colombia se desangró, una historia de la Violencia en metrópoli y provincia*, 1984); and coauthor of *A Reference Guide to Latin American History* (2000) and *Ten Notable Women of Latin America* (1978).

Mr. Henderson earned a bachelor's degree in history from Centenary College of Louisiana, and a master's degree in history from the University of Arizona. He then spent three years in the Peace Corps, serving in Colombia, before earning his doctorate in Latin American history in 1972 at Texas Christian University.

Colleen Madonna Flood Williams was born in Buffalo, New York. She now resides in Homer, Alaska with her husband, Paul, and son, Dillon. Colleen has a Bachelor's Degree in Elementary Education, with an Art Minor. She is the author of more than 10 children's nonfiction books.